I0811592

IMAGES
of America

PORTSMOUTH ISLAND

On the Cover: Jesse Babb (left) is pictured with his daughter Jessie Lee Babb (center) and her friend Mildred enjoying some music on their porch. Jessie Lee Babb was the last baby girl to be born on Portsmouth Island. (Cape Lookout National Seashore.)

IMAGES
of America

PORTSMOUTH ISLAND

James Edward White III

ARCADIA
PUBLISHING

ISBN 978-1-4671-0592-7

Published by Arcadia Publishing
Charleston, South Carolina

Printed in the United States of America

Library of Congress Control Number: 2020939653

For all general information, please contact Arcadia Publishing:
Telephone 843-853-2070
Fax 843-853-0044
E-mail sales@arcadiapublishing.com
For customer service and orders:
Toll-Free 1-888-313-2665

Visit us on the Internet at www.arcadiapublishing.com

*This book is dedicated to my grandmother Lucy Beacham Gilgo,
who introduced me to Portsmouth Island, instilling in me a
love for the island and its history, culture, and people.*

Contents

ACKNOWLEDGMENTS

There is no way that a project of this magnitude could be accomplished without the help and support of many others. This was a massive undertaking, more so than I first realized. I could not have pulled this together without the help and support of the Cape Lookout National Seashore in which Portsmouth Island is located. Within the park, I especially wish to thank park superintendent Jeff West for his help and encouragement. Along with Jeff, I would like to thank B.G. Horvat, chief of interpretation, and Karen Dugan, park ranger. They have gone out of their way to make available pictures from the park archives and, at times, search for specific photographs.

I would like to thank Connie Mason and Rosanne Penley, who read through the entire manuscript, editing it and offering suggestions for improvement and making various corrections as needed. Their encouragement and support have been immeasurable.

I would like to thank Rosanne Penley, Ann Ehringhaus, the estate of Lucy Beacham Gilgo, and the National Park Service for allowing me to use photographs from their collections. I most especially want to thank John Klecker for revising my photographs and putting them in a format acceptable to the publishers.

To my grandmother Lucy Beacham Gilgo and my aunt Nina Mann Dixon, thank you for all the many hours spent telling me stories of Portsmouth Island. They instilled in me a love of Portsmouth Island that has inspired me to write and share the stories of Portsmouth, preserving its history and culture.

Finally, I would like to thank my wife, Nancy, for her help, constant support, and encouragement. She read the manuscript several times, correcting grammar and spelling as well as offering valuable suggestions to improve the book.

Key to image courtesies:

AE	Ann Ehringaus
CLNS	Cape Lookout National Seashore
JEW	James E. White III
JW	Jean Webber
LG	Lucy Beacham Gilgo
NCA&H	NC Department of Archives and History
OBHC	Outer Banks History Center
RP	Rosanne Penley
TW	Tim Whealton

Introduction

On January 7, 1971, "Seventeen men and four women braved cold wind and icy rain to attend Henry [Pigott]'s funeral in the Portsmouth Church," reported the *Carteret County News-Times*. "Henry was buried in the Portsmouth 'family cemetery,' where colored and white rest together because they lived happily together." Henry Pigott's death was not just the death of a single man, but the death of a way of life—the end of an era. For with his death, the last remaining two women who lived on Portsmouth Island were forced to leave their homes there, and thus came to an end a long story that began as far back as 1738. Left behind were only memories, hollowed-out shells that once were homes, ruins that once were lives, and stories that were rich in lore of life and traditions of the sea.

In 1738, Richard Lovat received the island as a land grant from King George II. The following year, he deeded the island to Thomas Nelson, who in turn deeded it to John Kersey in 1753. In that year, the North Carolina Colonial Assembly established a town on the north end of the island named Portsmouth, which was to consist of 50 acres of land to be divided into one-third-acre lots. The first commissioners for the town were Joseph Bell, John Williams, Joseph Leech, Michael Contanoh, and John Campbell. In 1756, John Tolson purchased the first lot for 20 shillings. He was later appointed as a reader for Portsmouth by the vestry of St. John's Episcopal Parish in Beaufort, North Carolina.

The village steadily grew, with eight structures appearing by 1770. In the 1790 federal Census, there were 96 free white men, 92 free white women, and 38 slaves. By 1860, the total population of Portsmouth was nearly 600 people.

The soil on the island was too poor to sustain major agriculture, so the people earned their living from fishing, oystering, piloting, and lightering. Most families had a small garden, a cow, perhaps a pig or two, a few sheep, and a horse or two.

The village continued to grow until the Civil War. In 1861, the Outer Banks of North Carolina were quickly occupied by Confederate troops, who established forts up and down the banks for protection of the inland areas and Pamlico Sound. By 1862, most of the area had been taken over by federal troops under Benjamin F. Butler's expedition. As the troops entered the area, large numbers of residents evacuated the Outer Banks and headed inland. Most of those residents, white and black, never returned after the war.

Those who did return to Portsmouth after the Civil War made their living primarily by fishing, oystering, and hunting wildlife. With the opening of Oregon and Hatteras Inlets in 1847, Portsmouth ceased to be a major port of entry for North Carolina. In addition to the decline in work, there was danger from frequent hurricanes. The worst storm of the 19th century was the August 16–18 storm of 1899, known as the San Ciriaco hurricane, which completely flooded the island, doing considerable damage. A number of families left following the storm. It was followed by major hurricanes in 1913, two back to back in 1933, and another one in 1944. They, along with the closing of the Coast Guard station in 1937 and the closing of the school in 1942, began an exodus from the island. Henry Pigott's death in 1971 forced the remaining two residents, Marian Gray Babb and Elma Dixon, to leave. In 1973–1974, the State of North Carolina purchased the island and deeded it to the federal government for inclusion in the Cape Lookout National Seashore. Since then, the Cape Lookout National Seashore has worked diligently to restore and preserve the village of Portsmouth as it was in the 1930s.

In the mid-1990s, The Friends of Portsmouth Island was formed and has been instrumental in preserving the history of the village as well as helping to preserve some of the buildings and homes in the village. Portsmouth Island is part of Carteret County, just south of Ocracoke Inlet from Ocracoke Island, and can only be reached by water.

One

Portsmouth Island from 1735 to 1900

The first 150 years on Portsmouth Island were a time of growth up to the Civil War, followed by a period of decline. The Civil War was a major influence on the island, with most of the inhabitants fleeing the federal occupation. Following the war, most did not return. Hurricanes such as those in 1844 and 1899 were major events that also led to large numbers of people leaving the island. Out of the one hundred slaves on the island in 1860, only one black family returned after the war. Before the war, lightering and piloting were major occupations. Afterward, most men made their living by fishing, oystering, hunting, and later, shrimping.

During the French and Indian War, the North Carolina General Assembly authorized the building of a fort, Fort Granville, on the northern end of the island facing Ocracoke Inlet. This was to replace the old wooden lighthouse that burned on Shell Castle. Gabions, large barrels filled with sand, were placed in front of artillery for protection from enemy fire. Today, the remains of some of these gabions can still be seen when the tide is low and the wind is blowing out of the south, away from the island. There are approximately 10 left in the water just a few feet off of the island. (JEW.)

This water pitcher belonged to John Gray Blount of Washington, North Carolina. He, along with John Wallace, owned and operated Shell Castle off Portsmouth Island in Pamlico Sound. Shell Castle was an island or outcrop, approximately 23 acres in size, and contained a tavern, sawmill, gristmill, ships' chandlery, and wharves. It served as a major lightering station off of Ocracoke Inlet. Pilots would come in here, have their heavy cargo transferred to lighter-draft vessels that could go over the shallow water, and then reload to go to ports on the mainland such as New Bern, Edenton, Elizabeth City, and Washington. (NCA&H.)

This is the grave of John Wallace, "Governor of Shell Castle." Wallace operated the island as a fiefdom with servants and slaves, a gristmill, wharves, and taverns. He died in 1810 and was buried on Sheep Island in the southern part of Portsmouth. (CLNS.)

This is the oldest house left on Portsmouth Island and was possibly built as early as 1790. It was often called the "storm house" because it had braces to hold it in place during storms. It had a large upstairs where people could retreat from flooding during a major storm. The house was in the Roberts family until it was obtained by David Ireland around 1859. The son of Earles Ireland and Matilda Roberts, he was a blockade runner during the Civil War. When federal troops invaded the island in 1861, most of people left. The federal officer in command did not burn the house because David Ireland and his father were Freemasons, as was the officer. By the end of the 1800s, Wash Roberts owned the property and lived there along with his sister Jonesie. Wash was a member of the lifesaving crew and a Freemason as well. (JEW.)

This house was built about 1850 by Robert Wallace and was later owned by Charles Wallace. It was then purchased by John Grace and Theresa Burgess Grace. The Wallaces were lighterers as well as pilots, operating in the channel. By the early 1900s, the house was owned by Walker Styron, who was a member of the Coast Guard station on the island. The house was used by several families during the hurricanes of 1933 as a storm house. Following the hurricane of 1944, the Styrons left the island for Oriental, North Carolina. (CLNS).

DESTRUCTION OF FORT OCRACOKE.

As early as the beginning of the War of 1812, there were efforts to build a fort on Beacon Island in the sound off of Portsmouth Island. By the time of the Civil War, there was such a fort in place, known as Fort Ocracoke, although it was in need of repair. When Fort Sumter in South Carolina was fired on and Pres. Abraham Lincoln called for troops to put down the rebellion, North Carolina seceded and sent soldiers to the Outer Banks to build and man forts for the protection of the coast and inland waterways. By late 1861 and early 1862, federal troops under Gen. Benjamin Butler occupied the Outer Banks. Butler captured all the forts on the coast and headed toward Ocracoke Inlet. The men holding the fort were heavily outnumbered. Realizing they had no chance of survival, they packed up, destroying what they could. They spiked the cannons and threw them into the sound. They then left the island for New Bern, promising to send for their wives on Portsmouth. When the federals arrived, they found no one there and the fort had been set on fire by the retreating Confederates. (JEW.)

In 1894, the new US Lifesaving Service station at Portsmouth was finished and opened for operation. There were a number of different station masters. Some were strict, and others were lax. There were many shipwrecks off the coast of Portsmouth, with the lifesaving crew rescuing them with courage and honor. In 1915, the United States created the Coast Guard and made the lifesaving service part of it. The Coast Guard was active on Portsmouth until 1933, when it closed the doors to the station. The building was reoccupied during World War II to observe German U-boats off the coast. After the war, the Coast Guard station was again decommissioned. (CLNS.)

This was the lifesaving crew about 1915. The crew was under the supervision of Capt. Charlie McWilliams, who is probably the man at center. It is not known if this was the Lifesaving Service crew or the Coast Guard crew. (CLNS.)

Two

Portsmouth Island from 1900 to 1941

The period from 1900 to 1941 saw a continued decline in the population of the island. The hurricanes of 1899, 1913, and 1933 were all severe, causing much damage. As a result, more and more residents left the island. In 1937, the Coast Guard shut down its station, forcing men to leave for the mainland in search of jobs. By now, the major occupation of the men on the island was fishing, oystering, and crabbing.

The lifesaving stable was where the Lifesaving Service kept horses for the station. The horses were necessary to pull the lifeboats to the beach, and were also used to ride the beaches, monitoring for signs of a ship in distress. (CLNS.)

This is a surf boat drill at the lifesaving station around 1910. Lifeboats like this would be sent out through the surf to rescue the people aboard ships in distress in the ocean or sound. (CLNS.)

Monroe Gilgo (left) and Mitchell Hamilton were members of the lifesaving station. Based on their uniforms, they appear to have been part of the US Lifesaving Service. Gilgo was the son of William Gilgo and Emeline Robinson. (CLNS.)

This is a member of the lifesaving station crew about 1915, likely a US Coast Guard officer. A photographer came through and took many photographs of Portsmouth Island around this time, many of which have not been identified. (CLNS.)

Here is another member of the lifesaving station crew who appears to have been part of the Coast Guard, most likely photographed in front of his home on Portsmouth Island. (CLNS.)

This was a member of the lifesaving station crew around 1915. Based on his hat, he appears to have been a part of the US Lifesaving Service, not the Coast Guard. (CLNS.)

The first Methodist church was built around 1840 on land sold to the congregation by Dr. Samuel Dudley and his wife, Susan. It lasted until the 1899 storm completely destroyed it. The church seen here is the second Methodist church, built shortly after with the help of the people of Portsmouth working together. This church was destroyed by the hurricane of 1913. (CLNS.)

The schoolhouse seen here served the children of Portsmouth Island for many years until around 1925, when a new school was built closer to the village. It was a one-room building with a wood-burning stove. Children from grades one through seven attended. Originally, students only went to school for three months a year until the school year was extended to six months. The school year was later extended to nine months. (CLNS.)

This is the only known photograph of the class of 1916, taken at the old school. From left to right are (first row) Charlie Salter, Allie Ricci, Lionel Gilgo, Elmo Gilgo, Russel Dixon, and Ernest Salter; (second row) Elsie Salter, Leona Babb, Etta Babb, Viola Dixon, Madeline Harris, Ethel Gilgo, Estella Dixon, and Virginia Salter; (third row) Neva Salter, Verona Roberts, Mary Sneed Dixon (teacher), and Mabel Salter; (fourth row) teacher Mary Sneed Dixon, Alvin Harris, Tom Gilgo, Levin Fulcher, Henry Babb, Jim Gilgo, and Nora Roberts. (CLNS.)

Mary Sneed served as the teacher in the one-room school and later in the new school longer than anyone else. She married Abner Dixon, who lived on the island. They lived here until 1944 when the school was closed, moving to Salter Path where she continued to teach. She is pictured below with two of her students and an albatross at the school. (Both, CLNS.)

These appear to be the same two students in the previous image at school with the same albatross. (CLNS.)

The *Message of Peace* was a "booze yacht" or "rum runner" during Prohibition, bringing illegal alcohol into the country. The ship was carrying such a cargo when it ran aground off Portsmouth in 1923. This picture was taken by Lucy Beacham, a school teacher on Portsmouth at the time. (LG.)

This was the Northwest Point Lighthouse in Pamlico Sound. There was another lighthouse at the southwest point. They were built so that the lightkeeper could run the lighthouse and live in it with his family. This photograph was taken in 1922 by Lucy Beacham while she taught school at Portsmouth Village. (LG.)

The third Methodist church was built shortly after the 1913 hurricane destroyed the previous church. The money and materials were raised by Charlie McWilliams, keeper of the lifesaving station. He went to Ocracoke, Morehead City, Washington, New Bern, and anywhere else he could go soliciting supplies, materials, and money to rebuild the church. New Bern was a primary supporter of rebuilding the church. It opened sometime in late 1914. The author's mother was baptized in this church. (CLNS.)

This is another photograph of the third, and present, Methodist church. (CLNS.)

This is a close-up of one of the windows of the present Methodist church in the 1950s. (CLNS.)

Here is another view of the present Methodist church on Portsmouth Island, from the 1970s. (CLNS.)

This schoolhouse was built sometime around 1925 and replaced the earlier schoolhouse. It is closer to the village and consisted of one room, like the earlier school. The author's mother, Nina Gilgo White, attended this school when she was in second grade. Note the large water cistern at right. (JEW.)

This is the interior of the one-room school, showing how it looked when it was still in use. Note the teacher's desk on a raised platform. Copies of actual books used by students on Portsmouth Island are on the teacher's desk. (JEW.)

John Valentine "Tine" Bragg was born in 1836. He was married to Jane Ann Gaskill. They had five children: Caroline, Annie, Beaulah, Joseph, and Tom. (CLNS.)

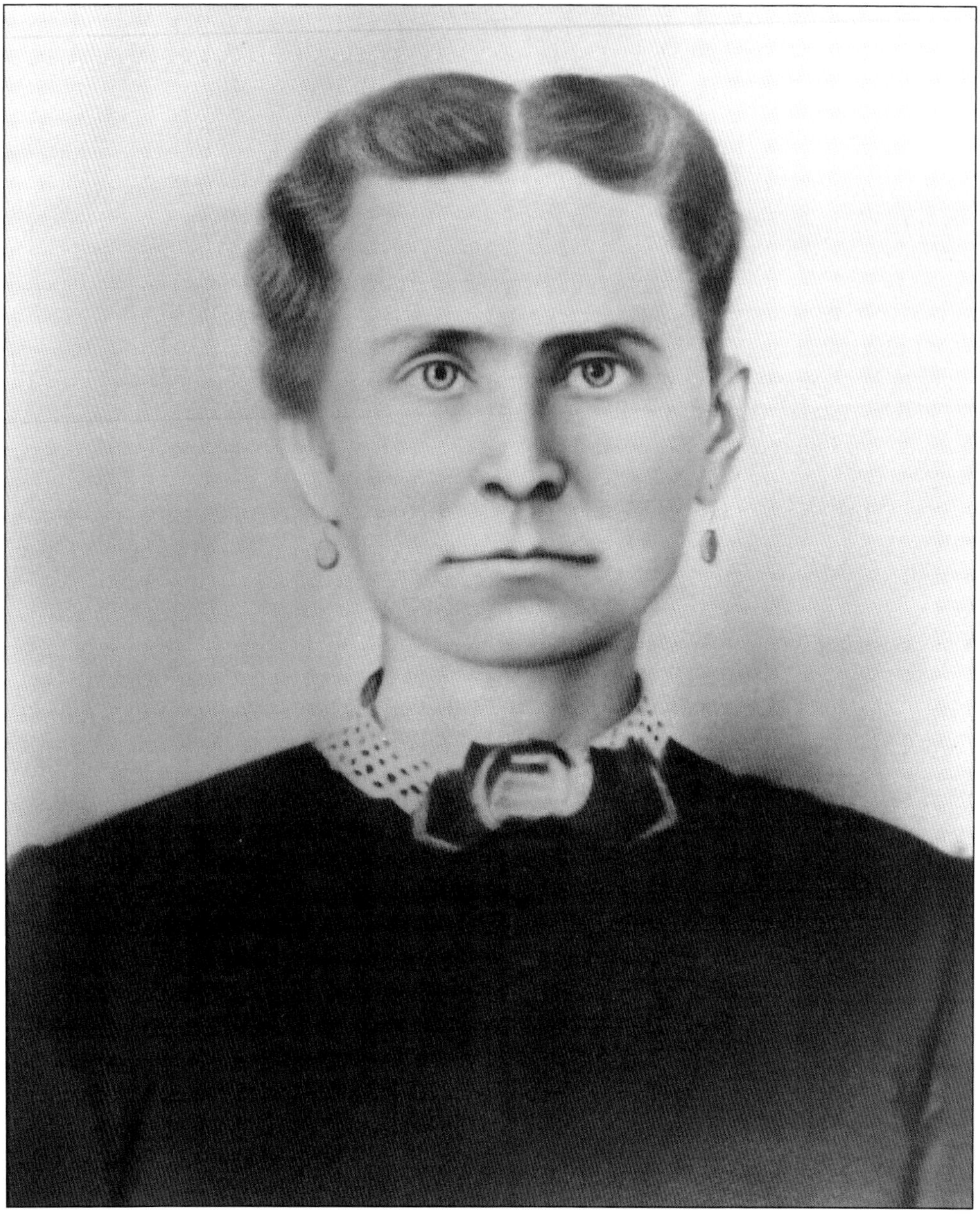

Annie "Hubb" Bragg was the daughter of John Valentine Bragg and married Jody Styron. Together with Tom Bragg, they ran a hunting club on the island. While Jody and Tom would take their customers hunting for ducks or pheasants, Annie would clean the house and cook for them. (CLNS.)

Beaulah Bragg was the daughter of John Valentine Bragg and Jane Ann Gaskill. She never married. (CLNS.)

Caroline "Line" Bragg was the daughter of John V. Bragg. She married George Gilgo and taught in the old one-room schoolhouse. (CLNS.)

Caroline Bragg and George Gilgo are pictured here in their later years. George was known for his live duck decoys and was a well-known duck guide on the island. (CLNS.)

This photograph was taken around 1915 along with the other pictures of Portsmouth. They may be a mother and daughter. (CLNS.)

One of the activities enjoyed on the island was a picnic or social. This event took place either at the Marine Hospital or the lifesaving station. (CLNS.)

This is possibly Claudia Williams in her later years. (CLNS.)

This young woman appears to be posed in the act of writing or drawing. (CLNS.)

Here is another Portsmouth Island woman, wearing a stylish outfit. (CLNS.)

Harry Dixon of Portsmouth Island is pictured here as a young man. He was the son of George Dixon and Martha Williams. (CLNS.)

Claudia Williams is seen here with her niece. Claudia was the daughter of John Williams and Esther Robinson. She married William T. Daly. (CLNS.)

Nora Dixon is pictured in her father's house about 1900. She was born in 1882 and was the daughter of George Dixon and Martha Williams. (CLNS.)

This picture was probably taken before 1920. (CLNS.)

Mattie (Daly) Gilgo was the daughter of William T. Daly and Claudia Williams and married Monroe Gilgo. Mattie and Monroe lived in the Middle Community, where she was active in the church and donated the piano. During the 1920s and 1930s, the Gilgo house became the social center of the island. It was here that the young people gathered several times a week for long walks across the beach. They would gather for parties, stirring up a big batch of chocolate fudge or congregating around the old player piano for a song fest. (CLNS.)

Lionel Gilgo is probably one of these two boys. (CLNS.)

Here are two young children on Portsmouth Island. Note the Coast Guard man in the background and that the young boy has on a sailor outfit. Also, note the similar haircuts on the two children. (CLNS.)

This is the only known photograph of Sam Tolson. He was married in Craven County, but his wife and child died in childbirth. He never remarried, living alone on the island. In 1865, he was arrested in Elizabeth City for the assassination of Abraham Lincoln, being mistaken for John Wilkes Booth. It took several people from Portsmouth to vouch for him to get him out of jail. (JD.)

A man and child play with a toy airplane. The airplane is on display today as part of the Cape Lookout National Seashore collection. (CLNS.)

This photograph was probably taken after World War II in front of Henry Babb's house. (CLNS.)

This family was photographed in front of the Babb house. (CLNS.)

This woman was photographed in the winter at the Coast Guard station. (CLNS.)

Here is one of the ministers from Ocracoke who preached on Portsmouth Island. The ministers were assigned to Ocracoke Methodist Church and came over to Portsmouth Island to preach on Saturday afternoons. (CLNS.)

The chimney at Casey's Island is the only remnant of the old menhaden factory on the island. (CLNS.)

This woman was photographed around 1930. (CLNS.)

This photograph was probably taken around 1930 in front of the Babb home. The Friends of Portsmouth Island have been working to restore this house. (CLNS.)

Pictured here are Henry Babb and Mary E. Dixon, parents of Jesse Babb. (CLNS.)

Here are three generations of Portsmouth Island men around 1935, with a little girl on the porch at right. (CLNS.)

These young people are visiting John Wallace's grave on Sheep Island around 1900. It was a popular place for picnics at the time. (CLNS).

Pictured from left to right are Ethel Gilgo, Lionel Gilgo, and Rita Gilgo, the children of Monroe Gilgo and Mattie Daly. (CLNS.)

This Portsmouth Island woman was probably photographed after World War II. (CLNS.)

Boatbuilding was not a major industry on the island, but many of the men did build their own boats, as seen here. (CLNS.)

Walker Styron was a member of the Coast Guard station. He left the island shortly after the 1933 hurricane. (CLNS.)

Milan Willis, son of Capt. David Willis, was a duck hunter, guide, and fisherman. He married Vera Gilgo, daughter of William Gilgo and Emeline Robinson. They had one daughter, Leida Mae Willis. (CLNS.)

Ethel Gilgo was the daughter of Monroe Gilgo and Mattie Daly. She married and moved to Morehead City. (CLNS.)

Jesse Babb (at left, son of Henry Babb and Mary E. Dixon), is pictured with his daughter Jessie Lee Babb (center) and her friend Mildred enjoying some music on their porch. Jessie Lee Babb was the last baby girl to be born on Portsmouth Island. (CLNS.)

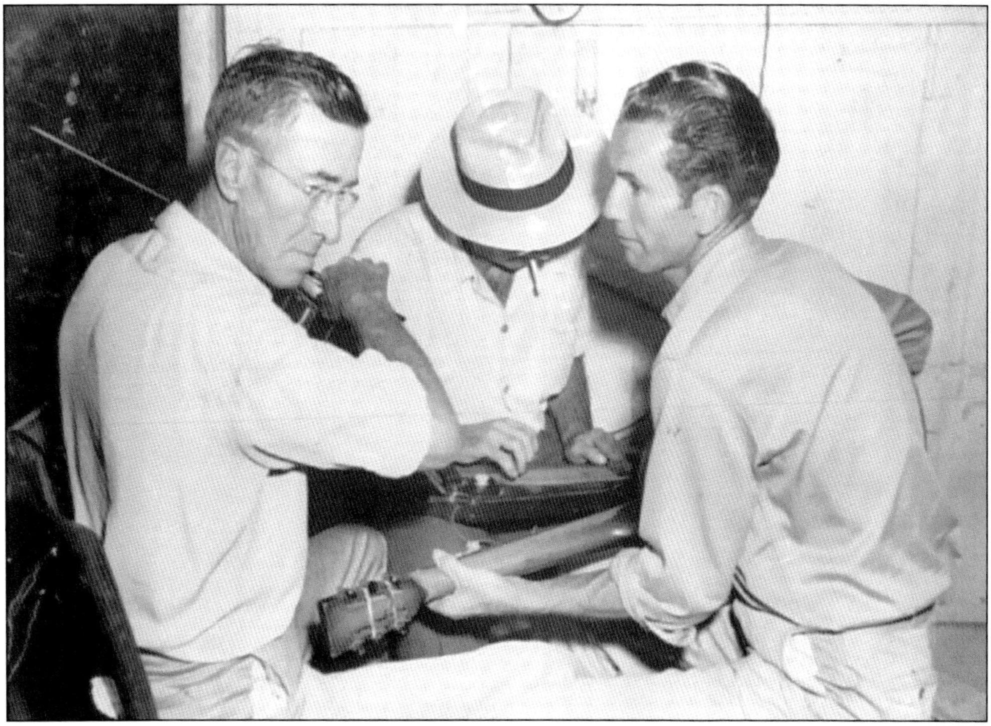

People on Portsmouth Island would play music on Saturday nights and hold square dances in the Marine Hospital until it burned in 1894. Then they held the dances in the schoolhouse. (CLNS.)

Elma (left) and Nora Dixon were daughters of George Dixon and Martha Williams. Elma was one of the two last women to live on the island, leaving in 1971. (CLNS.)

Washington "Wash" Roberts was a member of the US Coast Guard station and an active member of the Portsmouth community. He never married, living on the island until late in life. He finally moved to Oriental, North Carolina. (JW.)

Jonesie Roberts, the sister of Wash Roberts, lived with Wash in his house. She also moved to Oriental with her brother. (JW.)

Annie Salter served as the postmistress of the island in the 1940s and early 1950s. She ran the community store as well as the post office, which was contained within the store. When it was time for the mail to arrive, she would go home and change into a fresh dress and go back to the post office to put up the day's mail. (CLNS.)

This is Claudia Williams at her husband's grave. She was the daughter of John and Esther Williams. She married Capt. William T. Daly and continued to live on the island after he passed away. (CLNS.)

Taken around 1910, this family portrait contains several generations, which was normal for a family on the island. (CLNS.)

Three

Portsmouth Island from 1941 to 1971

The year 1941 signaled a new era for the people of the United States as well as for those on Portsmouth Island. The world was plunged into a great world war, and while many in North Carolina felt that the war was fought far from their shores, in fact, German U-boats patrolled the local coast on a regular basis. At night, the residents of Portsmouth could hear ships firing off the coast and see flames in the dark. The next morning, debris would wash up on shore, sometimes including bodies. To protect the coast, the Coast Guard station was reactivated. All windows on the coast had blackout curtains and residents were to observe strict blackouts at night to prevent German attacks.

In 1944, another devastating storm hit the coast, sending more people to the mainland. The school was closed for good, forcing those with children to leave the island in search of homes and livelihoods where they could send their children to school. As this period wound down, so did the population. By 1970, there were only three people left on the island who called it their permanent home: Elma Dixon, Marian Gray Babb, and Henry Pigott. In 1971, Henry died of cancer, leaving only Elma and Marian. Their families told them they had to leave the island, as there was no one left to look after them. So they packed up their things and their memories and moved to the mainland.

The Coast Guard station was deactivated in 1936, but when World War II broke out, it was reactivated due to German submarine activity off the coast of North Carolina. This is what the station looked like at the beginning of the war. (CLNS.)

This is a close-up of the Coast Guard Station at the beginning of World War II. There were not many changes in the station between 1936 and 1941. (CLNS.)

Pictured here is the crew of the Coast Guard station during World War II. (CLNS.)

A Coast Guard crew is dressed in their domestic whites for cleaning duty at the station.

This man served at the Portsmouth Island lifesaving station. (CLNS.)

The Coast Guard crew is at work placing a cement pad for a generator. The pad is still present at the station, but the generator is long gone. (CLNS.)

Members of the Coast Guard are pictured here on horseback at the station. They had a number of horses for patrolling the beaches, watching for German U-boats. (CLNS.)

There were wild ponies on the island at the time of World War II. Seen here is a roundup of ponies for use by the Coast Guard. (CLNS.)

This is another shot of the Coast Guard crew at the Portsmouth station. The photographer did not do a very good job of capturing the faces of all the men. (CLNS.)

Many of the Coast Guard men stationed at the island dated the Portsmouth girls, like this young couple. (CLNS.)

Here are two other couples on Portsmouth Island during World War II. At right is Edna Babb with her Coast Guard boyfriend Red. (Both, CLNS.)

Cars were rare on the island, but a number of residents had them. They were transported by ferry from the southern end of the island and driven up the banks. The photograph below is from around 1940. (Both, CLNS.)

Here is another car on the island, with a couple in the sand. The license plate appears to be from 1939, and there is a sticker from New Bern on the spare tire cover. (CLNS.)

This truck has been outfitted for fishing around 1950–1955. When the National Park Service took over the island, it had to remove a large number of old cars that had been left behind. (CLNS.)

Another car is seen here in the 1940s. A father appears to be letting his child pretend to drive. (CLNS.)

Four

Hunting on the Island

Portsmouth Island has always been a great place for hunting. The skies would often seem black from the ducks flying overhead. Guides would take men out hunting, and they would bring back barrels of ducks to ship home. Some of the buildings on the island were leased out for hunting clubs or lodges, including the Coast Guard station, the schoolhouse, and several houses. The two most famous hunters to come to the island were Babe Ruth and Franklin D. Roosevelt.

Jody Styron was one of the legends of Portsmouth Island. He was a guide who took people out on hunting trips for days. The trips would consist of duck hunting, pheasant hunting, or fishing, depending on the season. Tom Bragg and Styron had a house on the island where they could house and feed hunters and have their clothes washed. (OBHC.)

Tom Bragg, with Jody Styron and his wife, Annie, (Bragg's sister) lived in the same house and rented out rooms to hunters who came to Portsmouth. Annie cooked and cleaned the house while the men took their guests out hunting and fishing. (OBHC.)

A man and two boys pose, possibly after returning from a hunt. The man at center is holding a decoy, and there are three more stuck in the ground in front of him. (CLNS.)

These were live, tame decoys. In the 1920s and 1930s, a number of men raised and trained ducks with clipped wings to be used as decoys when they went duck hunting. George and Warren Gilgo were among the most famous for having trained live duck decoys. (CLNS.)

This is a tame decoy, one of many on the island. They were trained to sit in a pond or in the sound near the shore and call other ducks to them, allowing hunters to shoot the ducks flying in. (CLNS.)

George Gilgo is poling his lie-down waterfowl blind out into the sound. Clumps of marsh grass were laid on the flat deck, with the hunter lying down in the middle. Live decoys were stationed around the blind to entice wild birds to land. Gilgo was a regular duck hunter and served as a hunting guide on the island. (CLNS.)

Jody Styron is fishing off of Portsmouth Island. It appears he may be about to haul in a net. (CLNS.)

Men are seen here fishing on the Atlantic side of Portsmouth Island among the remains of a shipwreck. Today, Portsmouth remains a fisherman's paradise. (Both, CLNS.)

Two islanders display their catches of the day, which were not bad. There was a menhaden factory on the island in the latter half of the 19th century due to the large number of menhaden that could be caught off the shores of Portsmouth. Many of the men from 1865 on made their living by fishing. (Both, CLNS.)

Babe Ruth came to Portsmouth Island in the 1920s or early 1930s and hunted for a day. He is pictured above displaying a pheasant that he shot. Below is Tim Whealton (right), who was staying in the George C. Dixon home in the 1990s. (Both, JEW.)

Ben and Thelma Salter were well-known members of Portsmouth Island society. Ben ran the Salter Hunting Club, and was a well-known hunting guide in the 1950s. (CLNS.)

Perhaps the best-known hunter on Portsmouth Island was Franklin D. Roosevelt (seated in cart), who came to the island to hunt during the 1920s. (CLNS.)

Five

The Black Family on Portsmouth Island

In 1860, there were over 100 slaves on Portsmouth Island. In the face of federal forces occupying the island in late 1861 and early 1862, most of the residents fled to the mainland, taking their slaves with them. After the Civil War, most of the whites failed to return to the island, and only one family of former slaves came back. Those who returned had been slaves of Earles Ireland, and they came back to live with him on his property. A woman named Dorcus and her daughter Rose Pigott lived above the kitchen in a large room with a few other children. It is believed that Rose was the daughter of Earles Ireland because her children were recorded as his grandchildren in a later census.

The last man living on the island, Henry Pigott, who died in 1971, was a descendant of Rose Pigott.

Henry Pigott, seen on the steps of his home on Portsmouth, was a jack of all trades. He picked up the mail from the mailboat, fished and oystered for a living, and served as a maintenance man on the island. He was descended from slaves and was the son of Leigh Pigott and grandson of Rose Pigott. He was the last man to live on the island. (CLNS.)

This is another picture of Henry Pigott at his home on Portsmouth. He was beloved by the community and was buried in the Dixon-Babb Cemetery. (CLNS.)

Henry Pigott (left) and Walker Styron are pictured in Pigott's kitchen. Styron was a member of the Coast Guard and lived down the path from Pigott. Styron and his wife left the island after the 1944 hurricane. (CLNS.)

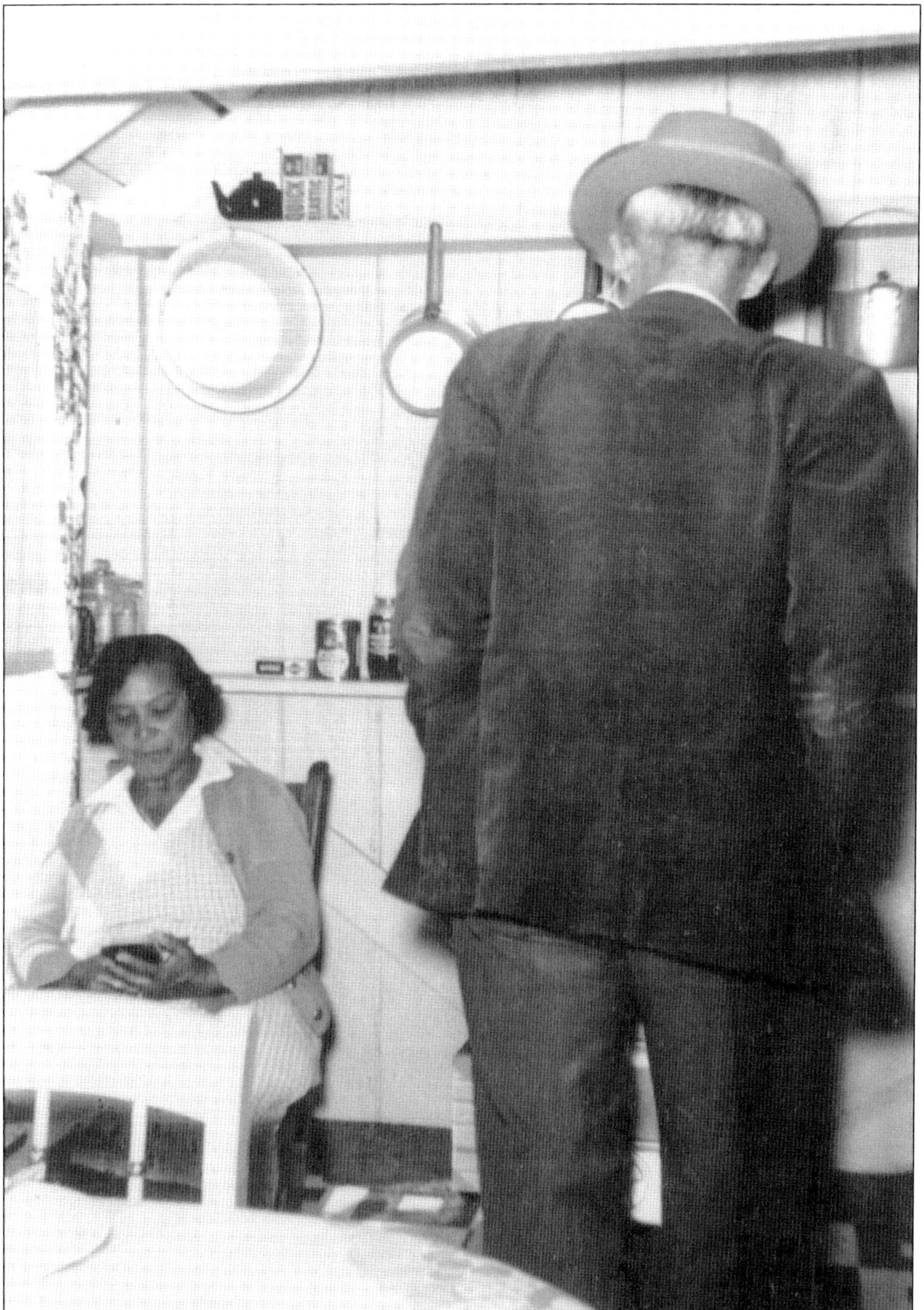

Lizzie Pigott was the sister of Henry Pigott and lived with him in his house on the island. Here, she is shown with Walker Styron. (CLNS.)

This is another picture of Lizzie Pigott (left) with two people of Portsmouth playing in the sound. (CLNS.)

Henry Pigott is shown here as a young man. (CLNS.)

Dorcus Pigott was the daughter of Leah Pigott and granddaughter of Rose Pigott. She married William Martin, who was a doctor in New Bern. Her father and his wife gave her a big wedding and reception on Portsmouth. His wife made Dorcus her wedding dress. (CLNS.)

William Martin grew up in Harlow and married Dorcus Pigott at Portsmouth. He was a well-known doctor in the New Bern area. (CLNS.)

Harriet "Hattie" Bragg had her father's last name. Her mother insisted that all her children know who their father was and carry their last names. She was the daughter of Leah Pigott. (CLNS.)

Olivia Martin Carter was the daughter of William Martin and Dorcus Pickett. She lived in New Bern and was the mother of Dorcus Carter and James R. Carter. (CLNS.)

Nettie Pigott was the daughter of Leah Pigott and lived on Portsmouth Island. She left the island as well, but it is not clear when, or where she went. (CLNS.)

Henry Willis was the son of Leah Pigott and had his father's last name. While he grew up on Portsmouth Island, he left to seek his fortune elsewhere. (CLNS.)

Lizzie Pigott was the daughter of Leah Pigott. She never married and lived with her brother, Henry, on Portsmouth. She too was descended from Rose Pigott and lived at Earles Ireland's place as a child. She cut hair for the people of Portsmouth, played the accordion, and sang. She was known for always having a lovely flowerbed around the house. (CLNS.)

Dorcus Carter was the daughter of Olivia Martin Carter. She became a well-known school teacher in New Bern, teaching for nearly 40 years. She remembered stories of the great fire of New Bern and often gave oral interviews of the fire and life in the 1920s and 1930s. (CLNS.)

James "Rudy" Carter was the son of Olivia Martin Carter and served as a Marine in World War II. He was one of the Mumfort Point Marines from Onslow County and was awarded the Congressional Medal of Honor. In his later years, he became very interested and active in the Friends of Portsmouth Island. Each year at the Portsmouth Homecoming, he rang the church bell calling the group together. (JEW.)

Following one of the homecomings, the author had the privilege to lead a number of the descendants of Rose Pigott to the cemetery where Rose and Leah were buried. The family also visited various places on the island connected with their history, including the houses where Dorcas, the slave, lived and where Earles Ireland lived, as well as Henry Pigott's house and the location of the old windmill where Rose and Leah worked. (JEW.)

Six

Cape Lookout National Seashore

When the last people on Portsmouth Island left, the State of North Carolina began to buy or condemn property on the island in order to keep it out of the hands of developers and to preserve it. After the state purchased all the property, including the village, it turned the entire island over to the Cape Lookout National Seashore, which had been formed in 1966. The Cape Lookout National Seashore is a 56-mile stretch of the Outer Banks, much of which has been left in its natural state. Other than Portsmouth Village and the Cape Lookout Lighthouse, most of the rest of the island is pristine.

Jeff West is the superintendent of the Cape Lookout National Seashore, having taken the position in May 2017. He is an active participant in park activities and has worked hard to preserve and restore the houses and buildings of Portsmouth Village, often seen in the village mowing the grass. (CLNS.)

Cape Lookout National Seashore was established in 1966. Its headquarters is at 1800 Island Road, Harkers Island, North Carolina. Tours to Cape Lookout can be taken from there via a short boat ride to the lighthouse and visitor center. The headquarters houses all the major offices of the park as well as books, videos, and audio recordings of Portsmouth. (CLNS.)

The interior of Cape Lookout National Seashore headquarters has displays on Portsmouth Island, Cape Lookout Lighthouse, and sea life of the national seashore. In addition, it contains a gift shop where visitors can purchase books, postcards, and souvenirs. (JEW.)

The Cape Lookout Lighthouse is across the sound from the national seashore headquarters. A short ferry ride takes visitors to the lighthouse and the ocean beyond. The lighthouse and keeper's quarters are open daily and staffed with volunteers. The lighthouse was built in 1859 and is 163 feet tall. It was fully automated in 1950. People are allowed to climb the lighthouse at certain times of the year. (CLNS.)

South of the Cape Lookout Lighthouse is the Cape Lookout Coast Guard station. It was established as a lifesaving station but became part of the Coast Guard when the Coast Guard was formed in 1915. The station is well preserved and kept in shape by the national seashore staff. (CLNS.)

The Cape Lookout Coast Guard station was decommissioned in 1936. It was recommissioned in 1941 for service during World War II. The station is pictured here during the war. (CLNS.)

This is another photograph of the Cape Lookout Coast Guard station. (CLNS.)

This is another photograph of the Cape Lookout Coast Guard station during World War II. It was manned during the war to search for German U-boats patrolling the coast of North Carolina. (CLNS.)

The Coast Guardsmen were on the lookout for American merchant ships sunk by German U-boats so they could rescue the crews. (CLNS.)

In this image of the Cape Lookout Coast Guard station during World War II, note the 48-star flag flying from the flagpole. (CLNS.)

Seven

Friends of Portsmouth Island

The Friends of Portsmouth Island (FPI) was organized in late 1989 to provide assistance and support for the Cape Lookout National Seashore. They help with preserving the history and culture of the island and have taken on the project of restoring the Henry Pigott house. They are now in the process of restoring the Jesse Babb House. They co-sponsor an island homecoming every two years on even-numbered years. The first island homecoming was on October 19, 1980, with regularly scheduled homecomings beginning in 1992.

The board of directors of the Friends of Portsmouth Island serves as the governing body for the FPI. They sponsor a number of projects, such as restoring the Henry Pigott house and the Jesse Babb house. Their major project is organizing the island homecomings every two years. (JEW.)

These are some of the members of the Friends of Portsmouth Island who come in during the week of homecoming. They spend their time sprucing up the island and getting everything ready for the homecoming events. They spend several days of their own time and money in order to get the island ready. Homecoming is a time of renewing friendships and making new friends, as well as telling stories about life on the island and preserving its culture. (JEW.)

After several long years of work by members of the Friends of Portsmouth Island, Henry Pigott's house was ready to open to the public. Here, the officers of FPI and the superintendent of Cape Lookout National Seashore are dedicating the house during a formal grand opening. (JEW.)

Henry Pigott's house is seen here after restoration. It was built about 1910. Henry and his sister Lizzie lived there until his death in 1971. (JEW.)

Henry Pigott's kitchen has been restored to its appearance in 1935, with authentic antiques. (JEW.)

This is Henry Pigott's bedroom. The room has been furnished with authentic antiques of the 1930s. The original bed was destroyed by Hurricane Dorian in 2019. (JEW.)

Friends of Portsmouth Island has taken on the project of restoring the Jesse Babb House for use as a work base for the members of FPI when they come to the island to work. Jessie Lee Babb was the last baby born on the island and was born in this house. (JEW.)

FPI members are seen working on restoring the Jesse Babb House. This house will be used by the members when they go to the island to do restoration work or prepare for homecoming. (Both, RP.)

Members of the Friends of Portsmouth Island are shown working on the Jesse Babb House. The roof had to be repaired as well as siding. The interior had to be repaired as well as painted. (RP.)

This is the bedroom of the Jesse Babb House after restoration. It, along with the other rooms of the house, has been filled with appropriate antiques of the 1930s and 1940s. (RP.)

One of the major functions of the Friends of Portsmouth Island is its biannual homecoming, which brings as many as 500 descendants and friends to the island every two years. One of the highlights of the event is the group picture, like this one taken in 2010. (AE.)

Another highlight of homecoming is the hymn sing in the church. As many as possible gather in the church to sing old hymns taken from the church hymnal. (JEW.)

What would homecoming be without food? There are usually six or seven tables loaded down with food of all types brought over by those attending from Ocracoke, Cedar Island, and the mainland. (JEW.)

About the Author

James Edward "Jim" White III grew up in Cove City, North Carolina, and graduated from high school in 1967. He went on to graduate from Louisburg College and the University of North Carolina at Chapel Hill with a bachelor of arts in history and political science. He then moved on to get his master of arts in education and later his education specialist degree from East Carolina University in Greenville, North Carolina.

He has published books on Portsmouth Island, New Bern during the Civil War, two Masonic lodges in New Bern, and a history of Cove City. He has received numerous awards for his writing from the North Carolina Society of Historians, including the President's Award.

Currently, Jim sits on the board of directors for the Friends of Portsmouth Island and on the board of directors for the Pamlico County Historical Association.

Jim is a retired teacher and has served as principal of Tyrrell Elementary School in Columbia, North Carolina, and at Bridgeton Elementary School in Craven County. After retiring from teaching public schools, he went on to teach at Pamlico Community College and at Mount Olive University.

He is married to the former Nancy Brinson. They have three sons and six grandchildren. (JEW.)